HOW TO LIVE YOUR BEST LIFE NOW

HOW TO LIVE YOUR BEST LIFE NOW

What You Need to Know and Do to Transform Your Life, At Any Age

FABRAYE FISHER MUHAMMAD

Fabraye Fisher Muhammad
How To Live Your Best Life Now

Published by Spines
ISBN: 979-8-89569-070-3

CONTENTS

INTRODUCTION

This book springs from a candid conversation I had with myself around 2 a.m. one humid morning in June of 2024. Seated in front of my laptop, that intimate discussion ended with the decision to throw apprehension to the wind. I was determined to complete, publish, and promote the book that had been stirring in my heart for what seemed like forever and just see what happens. The happening I presumed would be a new world opening up for me; one with the potential to assist others who, like myself, desired to live their best life now.

My morning reflection spanned the past three decades of my life. They had been what I would call 'eventfully boring.' There were joys, excitements, and achievements. I had loved and survived loss; raised children who were now young adults; earned a college degree; experimented with careers; lived in a few different cities; and traveled internationally once. In retrospect, I might have done some things differently. But, I surmised that I made the best choices given the information, resources, and understanding I had at the time. So, no judgments and no regrets.

But, in my heart, I expected that my life would have yielded more; specifically, more security and peace of mind. At that moment, I felt uneasy. Perusing my feelings, I realized that I was unconsciously worried. My concern was having an uncertain future; one governed by the whims or calculations of others; one where I might wake up and feel the same way 10 years from now. That possibility was as scary as the recent revelation of my hypertension. It was almost as petrifying as the classification of my condition as chronic.

My prolonged sleep apnea and the lack of energy and exercise maintained unwanted pounds. The result was a weakened immune system and my current health experience. But, the thought of having to take prescription medication for the rest of my life was unappealing and unacceptable. With some awareness of manifestation techniques, I knew there was another way to resolve this problem. I figured that just as I had created ill health, I could likewise re-create a healthy state of mind and body.

Accepting my current condition, allowed me to properly assess it and choose an alternative outcome; one with better health and without prescriptions. I was determined. Within a few weeks, my already low dosage was decreased by half and soon after halted altogether. I felt blessed to be free of medication. This health scare inspired me to make the remaining decades of my life more vibrant and fulfilling. The next step was a lifestyle overhaul.

The saying "Dissatisfaction brings about a change," rang true in my case. I was sick and tired of being sick, tired, and broke to boot. In the past, I worked to live as best I could, pay bills, and get by. Wealth was never a priority. Writing for the joy of it had been put on the back burner; set aside for when I had more time and resources. But, that time had not come, and life's clock kept ticking.

They call high blood pressure 'the silent killer.' But, the smoking gun behind my hypertension was the lack of fulfillment. I had failed to embrace my authentic self and was living a lifestyle that no longer served my highest and best interests. The way I was living was killing me. I was at a crossroads in my life -- Either continue to settle for a less-than-awesome existence or make some drastic changes.

I knew that there was a more simplistic way to navigate the complexities of human life. Years ago, I had asked into the ethers for a method, a blueprint on how to live better. Over time, I jotted down and refined the process that came to me. I intended to one day compile the partially completed draft manuscripts into print to help people improve their lives. That one day was now, and I was 'the people' who needed this process.

I realized that selfishly, I was writing this book for myself. However, unselfishly, I am sharing it with whoever resonates with it. Each of us is the author of our life's story. This process inspired me to start a new chapter in my life; one where writing and feeling good are priorities. The contents of this little book changed my life. It can do the same for you. Apply the process, enjoy the journey, and expect to feel better and **live your best life now.**

SECTION I

THINGS YOU NEED TO KNOW

Regardless of your current biological age, imagine that you are a child. You have loving parents, family, and a community of cheerleaders hell-bent on supporting you in whatever expression of greatness you choose, without judgments. They happily facilitate your growth through resources, and compassion with honest, heartfelt advice as needed. This is the ideal, but not every child's experience.

Most of the habits that we have as adults begin from early childhood. How we respond to advice, criticism, anger, and even love is programmed into our unconsciousness based on prior experiences. The good news is that even if your childhood sucked and your life is far from stellar today, you know the person who can change your reality. Just look in the mirror. It's you.

Consider this little book as your guide. It will arm you with the information and tools to consciously create a more desirable life regardless of your current circumstances. This is the beauty of universal knowledge and the practical application of it. The power of your intention trumps pre-determination, fate, or destiny. It supersedes seemingly external limitations. The proof is in the fact that you are reading these words now. At some point, you became dissatisfied with an aspect of your life. You desired change so earnestly that this little book made its way to you.

The process shared here is not the only way to change your life but, it is an awesome start. It holds a key, that missing link required for you to move to the next fantastic phase of your life's journey. Sometimes, it only takes a word, one phrase, or a paragraph arranged just right to spark that a-ha moment of clarity within. And, from that moment, you can see life differently. Possibilities that weren't apparent, appear. Hope springs true, and energy is renewed. This is my wish for you.

This is what life is all about; the journey of continuous phenomenal experiences that lead to growth and awakened consciousness. You, your Higher Self, is that consciousness. In truth, everything you need to be your best self, you already have. Here, you will learn one way, a simple process, to help tap into that Self and begin to live your best life now.

CHAPTER 1

KNOW YOURSELF

Awakening begins with knowledge of self. When you know who you are, others' thoughts about you become moot. Your feelings about whether someone likes or dislikes; agrees or disagrees with your lifestyle choices will no longer affect your choices. Self-knowledge is so powerful. It allows you to excel beyond the obvious factors of ethnicity, gender, religious affiliation, or cultural and social standing.

True self-knowledge is about self-definition. Understand this - Regardless of the life experiences you have enjoyed or endured to this very moment, you have the authority to alter your entire existence. When you know who you are, you can determine what is real. Your perception of reality is what allows you to determine your truths and avenues for self-expression.

Knowledge of self means that you, better than anyone else, know who you are. As a starting point for self-definition, understand that you are directly connected to the creative energy of all that is, was, or ever will be. You need to know this. You are more than the color of your skin, hair, or eyes. You are more than the gender you chose to incarnate or the family and culture you were born into. You are divine.

People are sometimes afraid to view themselves as divine. You may feel like you're being arrogant or thinking too highly of yourself. This is not about comparisons. Every human being is innately divine. To downplay who you are in the interest of false humility is to deny the essence of all creation. You are a magnificent part of the grand design. However, you, like most human beings, are living far below your true ability. This is due primarily to a lack of knowledge of self.

Accepting that you are divine can require a change in mentality. Your current living conditions may trick you into believing that you are less than divine. You might say to yourself, "If I am divine, like God, then why am I sick, broke, or unhappy?" You may be ashamed to accept who you are because of the life you have already created. But, the lack of proper self-knowledge leads to ignorance. Being ignorant is not something to be ashamed of; only staying that way is. Ignorance does not have to be chronic.

Without this self-knowledge, a person can be weak-minded, easily manipulated, and more likely to live a pathetic existence governed by the whims and insanities of self, or corrupt-minded individuals who desire to devalue and subsequently control humanity. Remaining uninformed about your true knowledge of self makes you potential prey and powerless. Knowledge is power. Power can be used for the positive or the negative.

Self-knowledge is enlightening. To know that you are one with infinite intelligence, the most all-powerful energy that exists everywhere, is energizing. You are pure, positive energy. When you know who you are, you can say, "Be and it Is." Knowledge of self allows you to ignite your power to not only exist and survive but to thrive, in a Godly manner.

More clearly stated: You are God, connected to the infinite energy of all that is. Because of who you are, you have the power to create in God-like magnitude. What seems like miracles, can become part of your normal existence. Now that you are clearer about who you are, let's consider why you are here, your purpose, and your reason for existing.

CHAPTER 2

KNOW YOUR PURPOSE FOR EXISTING

How many times have you asked yourself, "Why am I here?" This is a common human conundrum, but one with a simplistic answer. While I believe that every person has unique ways of self-expression, I also believe that human beings share a primary purpose for existing. You were born into human form to enjoy the process of living.

You came from a formless, spirit state into matter to explore the best that this sensory experience has to offer. Your spiritual, eternal, conscious self, opted to enter your current avatar for self-expression in this physical reality. I know this may seem far-fetched to some because you've been programmed to believe that enjoying life requires a trade-off. You were inundated with the slogan, "No pain, no gain." The truth is that pain is a resistance to change. And, until you change your mindset about why you are here, life may continue to be a painful, disappointing, lackluster experience.

Repeat – You, we are here to enjoy living!

The simplicity of this truth is no less accurate than understanding and accepting the fundamentals of human anatomy. It could be explained simply or with exhaustive detail. Rather than understand the complexities of how the body's heart, lungs, stomach, kidneys, and liver operate, it can simply be described this way, "The human body is a system of interconnected organs, tissues, and cells working together to sustain life."

Likewise, rather than agonize over your purpose for being, keep things simple. You were blessed with a body. Simplified, the process was that you were one among millions of sperm cells that successfully made the journey into and from your mother's womb into human form. That journey was as taxing and complicated as human existence ever needs to be. Now that you are here, be grateful and learn how to live simply and enjoy the moments. Understanding your purpose and the powers that you possess, serves to enhance your experience on Earth.

CHAPTER 3

YOU ARE POWERFUL

You now know who you are and why you're here. You should also know that you came here with powerful tools to assist in navigating your life. The magnitude of **your power is infinite**. When it comes to designing and living your best life, there are three primary powers that you must embrace and cultivate. These are the powers of choice, change, and creation. Rightly activated, these powers will allow you to master and express the best of yourself to the world. We start with the power of choice.

THE POWER OF CHOICE

Consider 'choice,' as a verb, an action word. To choose is 'an act of selecting or making a decision when faced with two or more possibilities.' Life is filled with options and experiences that require us to make multiple choices daily. Some choices are of more magnitude than others. But, every choice comes with a consequence.

If you're reading this now, you've had sufficient experiences with choices and repercussions. Take a moment and revisit what you would consider a great choice that you have made within the last year or so. Just the thought should make you feel good. Now, think of a time when you made a choice that gave you the opposite feeling. These outcomes are consequences of choices. The goal here is to be mindful of your ability to increase the amount of desirable outcomes in your life.

Sometimes having too many options can feel overwhelming. On the other hand, having too few alternatives can ignite the feeling of being trapped or stifled. In the best-case scenario, you have enough data and time to analyze a potential outcome. In other experiences, time may be of the essence, dictating that a choice be made in what seems like an instant. In this case, you must make the best choice based on the circumstances.

What you need to know is that even though choices come with consequences, they nor their resulting outcomes are inherently positive or negative. You just have to trust the process and know that regardless of your choices, "All things and everything work in your favor." No matter how 'bad' an outcome may appear if you're still alive, there is light at the end of the tunnel.

Granted, some extreme choices may result in harm to others, which can lead to grave consequences. This is why it is important to keep your mind clear and your energy in harmony with your higher self as much as possible. Feeling good about life and yourself produces an energy that leads to better life choices. Even determining when to and when not to act are choices. And when you know what you do not want, it becomes easier to determine what you do.

The beauty and power of choice is in knowing that **you always have one; a choice.** This knowledge enables you to be the director of your life rather than a victim in someone else's narrative. There are always alternative possibilities, or at least one. In any given situation, within the realm of time, circumstance, and your knowledge and ability; strive to **choose wisely**. This leads to your next power; the power of change.

POWER TO CHANGE

In addressing the power to change, we begin with the words of a dear old friend of mine, who has since transitioned. He would say, "Pain is a resistance to change." We had many heated discussions about this simple statement. However, over the years I have found his words to be true which is why I share them with you now. Consider this concept well. Wrestle with it and try to defeat it. The more you do, the more you will come to see the truth in its simplicity. And, the more you will be able to accept, direct, and utilize change in the most positive ways.

To change is, "to make someone or something different; to alter or modify." Change is a universal constant. Nothing stays the same. All living things alter over time. Believe it. When you know and accept the inevitability of change, it becomes easier to embrace the power within it. With this knowledge, you gain the power to identify and set trends within your life.

One way to better understand the importance of embracing change is to understand the benefits of it. Nature is a great example of this. Changes in nature help to create and maintain ecological balance. The natural events of floods and wildfires clear out old vegetation and redistribute nutrients which serve to rejuvenate ecosystems. Without these seemingly horrific changes, nature would become imbalanced creating a weakened ecosystem.

The same is true of human beings. As secure as a mother's womb is for her unborn child, the baby must be born to ensure its safety and the life of the mother. Thereafter, growth naturally ensues. Years pass and that same child makes changes on its own; changes fueled by choices. Depending on your desires in life, whether you choose to be introverted or extroverted; attend school, be self-educated or a combination of both; to be employed or self-employed; change is necessary for growth.

For certain, throughout life, you will transition from one state to another. When you accept change as inevitable and necessary, you will awaken this potential power within yourself. You can rise from the ashes like the Phoenix -- reborn and unstoppable, fueled by resilience and the power of self-reinvention. Properly used, the powers of choice and change can develop a more stable mindset that is less chaotic, more harmonically self-directed, and able to create on command.

POWER TO CREATE

To cause something to be brought into existence is defined as to 'create.' When I think of creating, one of my favorite movies comes to mind, "Harry Potter." It tells the story of not only the life of Harry but of an entire community of people with magical powers. They live in a different world, but parallel to normal, non-magical humans. Whether or not this type of world exists was never an issue for me. What fascinates me is the imagination that was used to create the story, from which the movie was thereafter produced.

The key to understanding the power to create is understanding that **Imagination Creates Reality**. Imagination is the 'faculty or action to form new ideas, images or concepts of an external object or experience not currently present to the senses.' More simply put, 'it's experiencing something in mind that has yet to appear in real-time.'

As adults, we tend to function according to habits learned as children. Unfortunately, parents and people in authority often tell children to, "Be real, stop dreaming, or get your head out of the clouds." At various stages of their development children are encouraged to stop believing. Adults say emphatically that the guests invited to a child's tea party aren't real. They say, "The dream to fly can't happen and that peace on Earth is asking too much." Without thinking adults tend to dampen a child's imagination. Eventually, children become programmed to agree with impossibilities.

The lack of belief in the 'impossible' dampens imagination. Imagination allows you to see what does not already exist. When you have an idea or picture of a thing in mind that you have not personally experienced, your imagination is at work. The moment you imagine a thing, it exists in your world as a virtual reality. Whether or not you choose to bring that vision into real-time for others to witness is up to you. When you accept that imagination creates reality, life opens and yields like a pearl from an oyster. Once you learn to wield your creative power it becomes yours to command at will. The power to create begins with imagination.

CHAPTER 4

TOP FOUR HINDRANCES TO SELF-ACTUALIZATION

The polarity of positive energy is the negative. Positive means, "that which moves you closer to your desires," and negative, "that which moves you further away." Consistent thoughts, whether 'positive' or 'negative,' form mindsets that attract similar energy and experiences. There are certain thought patterns with the potential to hinder progress more than others. They include doubt, fear, judgments, and inaction which are discussed below.

DOUBT

Doubt is a feeling of uncertainty or lack of conviction; a type of fear. It's a silent killer that leads to improper decision-making; low self-esteem and stress. When a choice is made and you second-guess yourself, over and again, the energy to succeed dwindles little by little until your original choice fades into obscurity. You forget about it, leaving the desire no longer charged with enough positivity to manifest as you desire. Doubt is a lonely feeling. You keep it inside because it's embarrassing to admit that you don't believe in yourself.

It is difficult to be confident when you doubt your ability to create favorable outcomes. Doubt is a cousin to low self-esteem. Closely related, both tend to rain on parades and trigger future disappointments. If you tend to think negative thoughts, decide to be more positive. As always, the choice is yours.

You can transform doubt into belief by reprogramming your thinking to be more positive. Start by changing your word choices. Instead of saying, "Don't run!" say, "Walk!" Rather than, "I'm not sure it can be done," say instead, "I expect success." If there are legitimate concerns surrounding a desired outcome, address them, fix them, and continue your motion toward a positive solution. Remember, words have power. They can affect your mood and mindset. Become more conscious of your word choices to help infuse more positive energy into your world.

Another effective way to relinquish doubt is

to incorporate daily affirmations into a routine. Start by repeating, "I believe in myself. I am positive, productive, and peaceful. All things and everything work in my favor." The results will be mind-changing and therefore, life-altering.

FEAR

Volumes can and have been written on the topic of fear. We've all felt fearful at one time or another. Fear has its place and value depending on the situation. But, seldom is it considered as a positive thought pattern. Fear is an unpleasant emotion caused by the belief that someone or something is dangerous, likely to cause pain, or presents a threat. Short of life-threatening occurrences, fear can be more rightly defined as, 'false, experiences appearing real." When it comes to changing one's life, fear can be a factor. However, out of proportion, it can immobilize you.

Mental fear becomes real when you think about it. In that moment, you are afraid even before something has happened. The fear of failure, success, or humiliation are such feelings; real or imagined. This means that you are suffering from self-inflicted mental anguish. Consider fear as a potential indicator rather than an absolute.

Whenever you feel fear, quickly put it into proper perspective so that you know how to best address it.

One positive way to deal with fear is to acknowledge it. State your fear aloud. Say, "I am afraid of failing; I am afraid of losing all of my money in this business; or I am afraid of starting a new relationship." Admitting your fears directly makes it easier to identify solutions for whatever you are afraid of. Maybe you fear becoming an entrepreneur because you feel that you don't possess enough experience or knowledge. The solution is to gain both. Once you have what you need to properly allay a fear, you can move toward achievement and success. Remember, most fears are illusions and will eventually become sparse to null as you grow in awareness.

JUDGMENTS

Everyone has opinions. People also have judgments, (an opinion about self or someone else's actions). Judgment usually involves adding a value opinion of positive or negative. Judgments can be from individuals and collectives such as communities, corporations, organizations, schools, and even families. Each collective has a specific culture of customs, norms, and behaviors.

Different cultures have varying views about how life is to be lived, and how success is defined within their sphere of influence. When you function within the boundaries of a given culture, you are judged favorably and rewarded with admiration and inclusion. Conversely, failing to live up to cultural expectations can lead to disapproval and even removal from that collective.

Related to lifestyle, judgment is associated with the appropriateness of choice. Judgments can be a strong hindrance to self-development. When you judge yourself for mistakes made in the past, or what you consider a lack of personal achievements, you minimize the benefits of learning from your experiences. You also create an energetic loop where you continuously repeat similar unpleasant interactions. The same is true if you judge someone else. In doing so, you connect with that behavior and to that energy. As you judge, you will also be judged. So the expression goes, "People in glass houses should not throw stones." Judgment is like a huge stone that drags down the spirit.

Remember, only in the present moment do you experience the past or future. Do yourself a favor and forgive yourself and others who may have judged you. Release the energy of judgments altogether. Dismiss the concept from your mind and accept others for who they present themselves to be. And, if a person's actions prove them to be other than what they purport to be, that's okay too. Truth always comes to light. Withholding judgment will open the gates of opportunity for you to encounter more enjoyable outcomes.

IN-ACTION

Doubt and fear lead to inactions and ill-actions. In a stagnant state you either do nothing or the wrong thing because stagnation functions on outdated information. In either case, the result is the same; disaster. There is a time to act and a time to be still. However, only with a clear mind, can you choose when and which action to implement for success. Failure to act when needed can lead to debilitating results.

The alternative to in-action is inspired action. Inspiration is that hunch or gut feeling that comes to you just when you need it most. It's that instinct that suggests you do or not do a thing. Inspired actions lead to exciting results; the kind that you just can't make up or orchestrate on your own. They lead to what people call miracles.

In-action keeps you a pawn in the game of someone else's world. Inspired action allows you to write your life's screenplay and be the leading actor. To combat in-action in your life, strive to function according to inspired actions instead.

With a general knowledge of who you are; a defined purpose; an understanding of your powers; and of how to transform hindrances into productive mindsets, you've laid a strong foundation. Now let's look at what needs to be done in preparation for **living your best life now**.

SECTION II

THINGS YOU NEED TO DO

Knowledge is power. However, dormant knowledge is just that, stagnant and unproductive until utilized. Once you've gathered knowledge, it's time to turn it into wisdom; the application of knowledge. This section is about applying what you know. Here we will discuss getting to know ourselves better, identifying what we value, and defining ways of fulfillment.

Let's get started.

CHAPTER 5

SELF DEFINITION

DEFINE YOURSELF FOR YOURSELF

We have already discussed who you are in a broader sense of understanding. You are connected to the essence of all that is, was, and ever will be. You are like unto God, a God; energy in human form that is infinite, but changes form through lifetimes. Attach to your current existence whatever name you are most comfortable with. But that is what you are called, not who you are. Naming is a part of self-definition, but not the beginning and end-all of your existence.

At birth, parents name their children. Names are words and words are powerful in and of themselves. Your name carries a certain vibration. However, as you define and express yourself, consciousness supersedes the energy of the name you are associated with. Feel free to rename yourself or give your current name a new meaning. Either way, know that your name merely identifies your avatar, the body in which you currently reside. It is not who you are.

"What does it mean to define self?"

One of the age-old queries of humanity is "Who am I?" As children, we look to our parents to tell us who we are. Who we consider ourselves to be often springs from our behaviors, experiences, and actions early in life. Habitual actions result from a mindset, which is influenced by cultural surroundings and repetitive experiences. This means that as children we are programmed into behaviors.

Childhood habits tend to perpetuate into adulthood. As an example, if you are scolded or worse for doing something, you learn to avoid that behavior or hide when engaging in it. Continuing in a certain behavior depends on whether or not, in your mind, the rewards outweigh the consequences. Children and adults share this behavioral pattern. Regardless of age, all actions have consequences. Behaviors that yield desired results with at least acceptable consequences, you consider as positive. Conversely, if a behavior results in an undesirable outcome, you will consider that behavior negative and are less likely to knowingly re-engage in it.

To make more conscious choices outside of the habitual childhood-learned ones, adults must grow to make more conscious choices. This is where self-definition truly becomes critical. When you know who you are in general, you become more open to reprogramming yourself as part of morphing into the type of person you desire to be. Self-definition is about how you present yourself to the world. At this stage, you are expressing your most authentic self. That self may be predominantly peaceful, analytical, assertive, or more reserved, organized, and introspective. You may choose to be some or a combination of many aspects.

But, when you understand the factors that contributed to your becoming who you are, you can make necessary changes to develop and present a more cohesive, integrated, and awakened self. You can then live more according to your prescribed definition of Self. Self-definition is also an expression of values.

DEVELOP PRODUCTIVE PERSONAL VALUES

Personal values are vital to self-definition. What three things are most important to you? These are the things that you value most. A value defined is, "a principle or standard of behavior; what is considered important or beneficial; the importance, worth or usefulness of a thing." Your values are a key aspect of self-definition. They speak to what you have chosen as the foundation of your being. They are what you believe. What you consider of value may change over time. However, your core values generally remain consistent, unless new information and experiences cause you to alter them.

Here we consider Personal Values as what you believe to be your truth. They govern behavior toward self and others. These values are personally consequential. Human beings have a strong connection to what they believe to be true. Keep in mind though, that having a belief does not make it accurately true or false, or positive or negative. Unless a belief leads to actions that are damaging to the life of another, no one has the right to judge another's beliefs.

Think about some things that you believe or believe in. Do you suppose that all people deserve to be treated with equality and justice? Are human beings connected? Should elements that sustain human life, such as earth, the sun, air, and water, be protected? These concerns may seem too huge to be considered of personal value, but what affects one affects the whole. Whatever you suppose to be true, or desire to be so, your choices and actions will support that belief.

Once your values are clearly defined, you will be able to recognize when you are in harmony or at odds with yourself. When in harmony, you'll make decisions more easily and feel good about them. Your level of surety will be high and communications more clear, concise, and in line with your goals in life. The next aspect of self-definition deals with fulfillment.

IDENTIFY YOUR WAYS OF FULFILLMENT

Fulfillment is a consequential component of better living. By standard definition, fulfillment is "the achievement of something desired, promised, or predicted; or the meeting of a requirement or condition." Regarding human development consider fulfillment as, "self-directed creative expression." Unless you truly know who you are and have clear personal values, almost everything that you desire to achieve is based on someone else's standards of success. Outside of basic human needs, most people, unfortunately, do not know what they truly want. This makes perceived desires more likely to be illusions.

True fulfillment is a euphoric feeling. It's a natural high, experienced when you are tapped into natural expressions of your abilities. When in the zone of fulfillment, you feel it and others experience your joy. In a fulfilling moment, there is clarity. It's like getting goosebumps or having an aha feeling of a light bulb pulsing in your brain. You know you are living your fulfillment when you are naturally high in the moment of doing what you love. It just feels right. It's what I am feeling right now as I write and edit these words.

The beauty of fulfillment is its diversity. There are as many ways of fulfillment as there are human beings on our planet. You could have the same passion as someone else but express it differently. Everyone is unique and like snowflakes or fingerprints, each person will express their talent as fulfillment in divergent ways. Some ways may seem more exciting than others, but none are any less precious. Fulfillment is relevant because it is a pivotal expression of individual consciousness.

I marvel at little things like paper clips, hair pins, cotton balls, and Post-its. People use these items daily but rarely consider their origins. What intrigues me is the fact that someone thought about and nurtured the concept of these items into existence. Because of these individual innovations, people all over the world are employed and supporting their loved ones in daily activities associated with making these items. It is truly amazing when you think about it.

The nurturing and development of one person's talent may bring them fulfillment, but everyone benefits. That's why one person's fulfillment is a blessing to many. Fulfillment is awesome! There are many ways to identify your particular vehicle for fulfillment. You may have more than one area, but I encourage you to start with one, preferably the one that is most obvious. For me, writing has always been a source of relaxation. It allows me to clear my head when needed, express feelings, and more recently share better living processes for self-development that anyone can benefit from. How does it get any better than this?

Sometimes identifying your talent is obvious and sometimes it's not. For some, you may have to dig deep down within to identify your particular spark. Start by asking yourself what things you are naturally good at. It's usually easier to identify gifts that are sensory such as singing, dancing, teaching, or artistic. Other talents like the ability to: deduce; translate complexities into simplistic understanding; organize or exercise dexterity, or learn languages are more subtle and require more insightfulness to identify.

You may have had experiences that help you to easily identify your talent. You may need to think back to your childhood to rediscover your gifts. Think about when engaging in an activity brought you joy. Whether it's clear as day or requires investigation to identify, it is worth whatever time and effort is required to pinpoint your fulfillment vehicle. Determining how you will express yourself to the world is an aspect of self-definition because your passion, gift, and talent are part of your Most Authentic Self.

SECTION III

3-STEP BETTER LIVING PROCESS

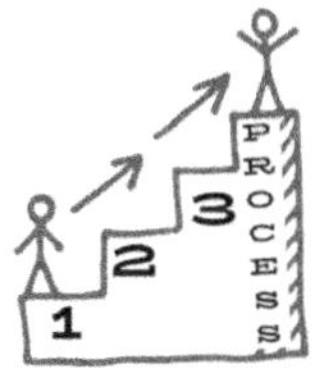

Expressing your God-self to the world is a benefit to yourself and humanity. Once you have decided how you will show up in the world and what contribution you will make, you'll need a proven process that yields optimum results when properly implemented.

CHAPTER 6

STEP 1, CLARITY

KNOW WHAT YOU WANT

When you know what you want you can have it. The exception is a desire outside of the realm of probability for your being. As an example, if you are 80 years old and want to be a premiere ballerina or gymnast, the probability is likely outside of your physical ability. Meaning, the realization of this choice would not be in your best interest. This may seem like an extreme example, but this is how astute the law of creation is. It works in your favor. If there is even the slightest possibility for a desire to manifest, it can, barring extreme extenuating circumstances that are not in your favor.

With that said, more likely than not, you can have whatever you desire. In this awesome world we live in, there are so many things to experience. The beauty of living is that as long as you are breathing, you have the opportunity to manifest almost anything that you desire. Learning and applying this process is the difference between living and surviving. As you move toward clarity, start with self-assessment.

SELF-ASSESSMENT

To get what you want start with an inventory of what you already have. As an example, if your desire is for optimal health, honestly evaluate your current state of health. Write this down, ideally in a designated journal so that you can chart your progress over time. A health-related journal entry might read something like this, "Currently, I have pain in my left leg and I breathe heavily after walking up a flight of stairs." Be specific.

Related to finances, you might desire more money. To accurately assess where you are financially, look into your bank account. Write down the quantity of funds in your checking and savings accounts. Find out your credit score. Make a list of your current assets, your average monthly income, expenses, and outstanding debts. Determine if your current income and job are to your liking. Honestly acknowledge how you feel about everything related to your finances. Do this same assessment for each major area of your life that you would like to improve.

Once these lists are completed, make a new list of things you are grateful for. Start with, "I am grateful that:

- I have a functioning body.
- I can make it up my stairs.
- I have a bank account.
- I live indoors.
- I have a regular income, etc.

Expressing gratitude for what you already have creates a positive energy that opens the pathway to receive more. Self-assessment does not require complex psychoanalysis. It merely requires documenting where you are in the major areas of your life; namely: **fitness**, **fulfillment and fun**, **financial abundance,** and in relationships with **family and friends**.

Your current experience in each of these areas is what you have created it to be. All of this can and will begin to change as you implement this better living process.

DESIRE

In one or more of the core areas, you may be at optimal levels. However, for whatever area you yearn to improve, list your preferred desire. To desire is "to have a strong feeling of wanting to have something or wishing for something to happen." Related to human development and manifesting a new reality, your desire needs to be a **burning desire**. Start by writing down what you would like to change. Then, review and rewrite your desire until it becomes more specific. If at any time, you find yourself struggling to narrow your focus, stop.

Sometimes, a desire can only become so specific before you begin to strain within the process. Attempting to force change can be counterproductive. The process of coming into clarity should be as simplistic as the blinking of an eye; not something you have to worry about. As you implement this process, clarity will organically flow from one stage to the next.

If you are not ready for change, consciously accept your current situation and make the best of it to help mentally release any tensions. This will gradually move you toward better energy until you are more certain about the new choice that you would like to make. Burning desire starts the ball rolling toward preferred change. With it, you place yourself in a better position to make conscious decisions.

DECISION

Desiring something is one thing, but deciding to have it is another. A decision is a preferred outcome born out of the process of evaluation. Decision-making can be as simple as what you will eat for dinner, or as detailed as the amount of income you will earn over the next few months.

Once a decision is made, the specifics manifest over time. Keep in mind that time is relative and in direct proportion to your level of applied awareness. The more you marinate on a new decision and focus awareness on it, the more related experiences will appear to help refine your choice. Remember, living is a journey, not a destination. When you enjoy the journey, you are more likely to be happy once you get to where you want to be.

The goal is to enjoy the process of living as it unfolds according to your desires. So, be honest about how your life is now; consider options on what you would prefer instead; then, fearlessly decide how your life is to unfold. This is the clarity needed to begin the process of transforming your life for the better.

CHAPTER 7

STEP 2, CONFIDENCE

ACCEPT THAT YOU CAN

Confidence is "to have a firm trust, the feeling or belief of being able to rely on someone or something." This step requires knowing that you deserve what you desire and accepting it with confidence.

To deserve is "to embrace qualities of being worthy of reward or punishment." The choice of what you deserve is up to you. This choice directly affects the outcome of success or failure in the attainment of your goals. If you say that you want something but secretly believe that you do not deserve it, you nullify your ability to receive it. Essentially, you are asking for something, but pushing it away at the same time.

Know this – As part of your birthright, you deserve all you earnestly desire. This is a spiritual promise associated with being born into this existence. The universe we live in is obligated to facilitate whatever we desire. Most people do not know it, but this realm, our world, is our facilitator. Think of it as your personal magic genie. Better yet, consider it as God unconditionally working in your favor.

Fortunately, knowing what you want does not require knowing how to get it. The 'how' is the work of universal consciousness. Think about it. Billions of people on Earth have a myriad of desires. The manifestation of these desires is like an intertwined web incorporating intricate steps and people to facilitate each desire. No one in their right mind would want the responsibility for deciphering the maze of activities required to fulfill everyone's wishes. So, rather than boggle your mind with every little detail, let go and relax into knowing. Trust that the Universe has got you. Know that you will be directed through inspired actions on which steps to take and when.

There is a difference between wanting something and accepting that you already have it. Acceptance is "knowing that a manifestation is a done deal; confirmed without doubt." This concept is basic but paramount. Simply put, acceptance is 'a conscious agreement to receive.'

Without it, no agreement exists between you, your desire, and the coming of it into real-time.

When you ask, it is given; instantaneously created. Be confident in this level of creation and you become one step closer to consciously realizing and sharing your desires with the world.

CHAPTER 8

STEP 3, COMMITMENT

MANIFEST YOUR DESIRES

As co-creators with the universe, everyone has free will to accept, reject, and choose almost any desired lifestyle. We never have to worry about being universally forced to conform to fate or destiny. Each individual creates reality according to predominant thoughts and feelings. The energy of consistent thought connects with its physical counterparts. Therefore, conscious manifestation requires a **commitment** to focus on your expressed desire.

A commitment is "a promise or declaration that a person will or will not do something." To live your best life now, commit to consistently enjoy focusing on your new desire. Commitment and habit go hand in hand. Habit is "regularly repeated, routine behavior that tends to occur subconsciously."

Focus requires silence. In silence, you can strengthen your ability to focus. Learn to just be. The regular practice of silence, meditation, or prayer puts you in the spiritual mindset to focus with ease. In a quiet space, it is easier to hear the voice within as inspired actions are shared or downloaded to you.

The world tends to be a noisy place. We are regularly bombarded with sensory distractions and electrical impulse disruptors. This can interfere with your ability to silence yourself. Consider silence as your workshop; the place where you consciously create. Your first commitment is to develop the habit of regularly spending quiet time with your desire. If you ignore your desire it will elude you.

You've probably heard this expression, "To get something, you must already have it." This statement boggled my mind for a long time because I considered it nonsensical. However, after many more years of questioning and experimenting with this concept, I now understand and appreciate it. These words are universal truth; unrefutable and unchanging. Understand this and you are another step closer to manifesting with intent.

The benefit of silence is melding into a state that allows for the ease of using your imagination. **Imagination creates reality.** Many writers and speakers share this thought. Imagination is "the formation of new ideas, images or concepts not apparent to the senses." To have an experience not currently available to the physical senses, you must have that experience within your mind, virtually.

Virtual means, "almost or nearly as described, but not completely or according to strict definition; not physically existing as such but made by software to appear as such." Our mind is like a computer program and our persistent thoughts are like the software. Imagination is your virtual world playground. Your consciousness uses its energy-infused virtual storyboards as content that will manifest into your real-time reality.

In the safety of your virtual world, anything is possible. Every desire exists now. They continue to manifest to the extent of your interaction inside of them. Knowing this makes you capable of saying, **"Be and it is,"** and for this statement to be immediately accurate.

In your virtual world, your imagination can run wild. You can be healthy; ski the Alps; climb

Mount Everest; exude wealth; and even be as wise as ancient sages. In your virtual space, you can be attractive, smart, and able to live your best life now. Your virtual reality is your game room for creating as desired. It is your fun space and the more time spent there enjoying your desires, the better you will feel. Feeling good connects you with other things and people who support that feeling. It also becomes easier for the universe to match you with your desires.

The commitment stage of this process is so much fun. Spending time in your virtual world is truly living your best life now. You don't have to wait. You get to experience your desires because you are encountering them now. Your imagination allows you to instantly be in the moment of your desires. The steps of Clarity and Confidence go hand in hand with Commitment. Combined you have a winning formula for success in all areas of your life.

SUMMARY

Creating virtually might be considered by some as a way to escape reality. On the contrary. Experiencing in the virtual is one of the best ways to manifest with intent. Most people create life experiences accidentally and habitually. In this way, sometimes you'll get what you want and at other times not. The failure to create as desired is due to a lack of understanding and the improper implementation of universal principles and practices. The simple, three-step process shared in this little book is foolproof. It works when you work it, according to inspired action.

To live your best life is to develop a lifestyle that is conducive to your highest quality of living while being your most authentic self. Living well is about more than just manifesting things. The pursuit of tangible, sensory objects alone is to live a **low-quality** life. This type of life can lead to a false sense of self where you are always searching for the next best thing. In this way, you may experience momentary happiness but fail to achieve the euphoria of lasting fulfillment.

High-quality living is when your four core areas of life are in harmonic resonance; where you are expressing yourself in the most fulfilling manner using your innate talents and gifts; and enjoying the process of doing so. A high-quality life is not generic. It is specific to the individual. But, it includes a balance of worldly and personal values; sensory possessions, and internal peace. Accept that life exists only in the now. The past and future exist only as you think of them in the present moment. Now is the time to experience fitness, fulfillment, fun, and positive relationships with family, friends, and all walks of life.

Recognize that life is a journey and that if your goal is merely to migrate from one manifestation to the next, then you are missing the point. You can be disconnected from a desire if you fail to enjoy the journey of getting there.

Live in the moment. The systematic pathway to realizing your desires starts with acknowledging the gift of the present. Choose the life you desire. Develop skills that you are passionate about.

Know that quantity does not define the quality of your life. Quality is in the fulfillment and enjoyment that you experience in every moment while consciously creating the life you desire. Truly living well is about how you develop and express your highest and best self to the world; preferably without self-judgment or judging others. Think positive thoughts. Acknowledge that the universe creates the best pathway toward the realization of your desires. Follow your inspired actions. Use your imagination and virtually enjoy your desire while it is manifesting.

Don't waste time worrying about what happened yesterday or what might occur tomorrow. Yesterday is gone. Tomorrow never really comes. Everything that ever occurs is only experienced in the present; right here, right now. The words you have read, and the process that has been shared, may seem too simplistic to be viable. But, as a dear friend said to me, "If you want to know if a berry is sweet, taste it." In other words, Be brave and put the contents of this little book to the test. Trust the process. At the very least, you'll feel better about yourself. At best, you'll become more aware and better able to consciously create a better life for yourself.

You manifested this book because you are ready for change. Now start from wherever you are. Do what needs to be done to alter your mindset. Take the time to implement this better living process, and choose to **live your best life now.** You can do it!

And, so it is.

ABOUT THE AUTHOR

Fabraye Fisher Muhammad is a multi-talented author in the self-help and personal growth genre. With a diverse background in law, journalism, videography, and youth development, she now brings her passion for writing to the forefront to help others be their best selves and live their best lives.

www.ingramcontent.com/pod-product-compliance
Lightning Source LLC
Chambersburg PA
CBHW070919160726
48004CB00003B/1440

* 9 7 9 8 8 9 5 6 9 0 7 0 3 *